MW00356425

Dedicated to the healing

and to the healers

Barry J. Schieber

Nose to Nose

A Memoir of Healing

Silent Moon Books

ISBN: 978-0-9721457-0-1

2002 COPYRIGHT © Barry J. Schieber

All Rights Reserved

FIRST EDITION:

Second Printing 2007

PUBLISHED BY:

Silent Moon Books

Post Office Box 1865

Bigfork, Montana 59911

E-mail: info@silentmoonbooks.com

www.silentmoonbooks.com

The Delta Society® and Pet Partners® programs are
registered trademarks of the Delta Society and are used
with the permission of the organization.

PRINTED IN CANADA

Contents

Acknowledgements

*"When eating fruit,
think of the person
who planted the tree."*

VIETNAMESE PROVERB

Once begun, this book took on a life of its own. I wish
to express my thanks: To Bob and Tina Denison, for
giving me their home, an ideal environment for writing.
To Terry Lahens, for her unending encouragement.
To Jonathan Swinchatt, for his kindness to man and dog.
To Carol Kanter, my childhood friend, who patiently beat
me over the head to "write already." Her compassionate
editing allowed the book to unfold. To the Delta Society,
for their ingenious program, and the staff and patients of
Community Medical Center, for their open-mindedness.

And to Moritz, for opening my heart.

Prologue

I was living in Lucerne for the winter, recovering from an unexpected illness. I had been traveling when — in the midst of the holiday season before the new millennium — I became sick. Suddenly I found myself a patient in the hands of a kind and capable Swiss doctor. He acted quickly to remove the cancer from my bladder, performing two operations over the next six weeks. After each surgery, I recovered for four days in a beautiful hospital overlooking Lake Lucerne.

Although I had a caring medical team and friends who visited me often, the hospital was a foreign land for me and I felt the absence of familiar surroundings, of home. Maybe that is why I found the lake right outside my window (not unlike my lake at home) especially comforting.

In March, I boarded the train for Geneva with my friend Andrea Röthlin to meet Don and Diana Kennedy, good friends from California who were spending a few days in Geneva. Don's invitation to come visit for the day felt like a spring tonic.

Don met us at the station and we walked a few blocks to his hotel on Lake Geneva. Diana greeted us in their hotel suite and we began to catch up. During the conversation I noticed a bowl with two goldfish sitting on a table. Don laughed as he showed me a hotel card that read, "Hello. Our names are Laurel and Hardy. Please do not feed us, as it is done routinely." I was amazed at the warmth these living beings added to an already beautifully decorated hotel suite.

I remembered their Bernese mountain dog and asked:

"How's Heidi doing?"

Diana's eyes filled with tears. "Heidi died last month. She was only four years old. We went out of town and boarded her with our vet. Her stomach bloated and she died before they could help her."

"I'm sorry." I remembered that Fritz, their previous Berner, had also died young and suddenly.

Don said, "We both agree that they were a joy. Those Bernese were the best dogs we ever owned. If we were ever to buy another one, it would be from a breeder here in Switzerland. I've lost my faith in American breeders."

Don must have agonized over their dogs' premature deaths. Still grieving, they had decided to wait before considering a new puppy.

Their sadness cast a shadow over the happiness of spending our day together.

⤟

Our meeting put the idea of getting a puppy into my head. Andrea's sister knew about dogs, so I asked her if she could find a good Bernese breeder. Two days later, Evelyn called to say she just met a man walking a beautiful Bernese. He gushed on and on about all the research he had done to find the right breeder, how the one he had finally chosen was the best, and — oh, yes — the breeder lived nearby, and his bitch had just had a litter of seven puppies. Evie took the breeder's phone number and address and gave it to Andrea to set up an appointment.

I was surprised, curious, excited — but I wondered what was I getting myself into. Was I really going to bring a puppy home to Montana? How would having a puppy change my life? I knew very little about dogs.

Well, in any case, a visit to see the puppies would be fun.

Andrea made an appointment for the next day. Pia and Roli von Moos live in a beautiful white home with red shutters on an Alpine hillside above the village of Flueli-Rauft. The village is famous as the home of Brother Klaus, the spiritual patriarch of Switzerland.

This seemed auspicious. When we arrived, Roli was hosing down the driveway. My first impression was "Such a friendly man" — and Wow, were his house and yard Swiss clean!

There was no sign of the seven puppies, or their mother, Deicha. Roli took us to the backyard to visit his new canine family. On the grass were small shelters for shade and toys for the dogs. The kennel was spotless.

Cuddled together were seven, eight-week-old Bernese puppies. Deicha was resting near the chain link gate. When we approached the gate, she barked a deep, loud bark that scared me and sat down. But when I got closer to her, I noticed her kind brown eyes. She was elegant, and she quickly became friendly.

Bernese puppies are irresistible. All had the markings that, as Don had told me, make them "designer dogs" — a white blaze on the face, a white cross on the chest, shiny black fur, white paws, copper brown legs, and a white tip to a black tail. I felt a thrill run up my spine.

The puppies woke up and began playing. One stood out as the alpha of the litter. He had a much larger chest than the others and was first to the food dish. He was already taken, and three of the others had homes as well. Of the three remaining, two were male and one was female. Each pup was wearing a different color identification collar.

It was a sunny afternoon, and before long Roli's two children were showing Deicha off by hiding food for her to find and getting her to do a few tricks. I could not judge her intelligence, but it was easy to see her nature — gentle, alert, protective, graceful, and obedient.

We began playing with the puppies, trying to select one. They all looked more or less alike to me. Only the colors of the collars saved me from utter confusion. Two puppies were calm and quiet, a male and a female, and both were available. When I picked the male up, he relaxed and simply rested his head in my arms. I set him down and he bowed, front legs extended, chin on the ground, a sway in his back, wagging his tail. He was ready to play. He chewed on my shoes, teethed on my finger, and rolled about on the grass.

"How big will he get?"

"It is hard to say. Look at the size of his father."

Roli pulled out an album and showed us a photo of the puppies' father, Amadeus, a large, stately Bernese who was a Swiss/German/Dutch champion. He was much larger than Deicha, who was considered too small to be a champion.

"Is he as gentle and good-natured as Deicha?"

Roli smiled.

"He had a good time while he was here and seemed to be intelligent."

"Any hip problems?"

"One cannot be sure about his grandparents and great-grandparents; but both his parents do not have problems."

Roli opened the album again to show us more pictures of Amadeus, of Deicha, of a visit to the vet that showed Roli's children pointing to the seven embryos on an X ray. Finally there were photos of the birth of the puppies and the first "family" photo with Deicha.

By the time we had finished going through the album, we felt as if we had become part of Roli's family.

Roli turned over the puppy's earflap.

"Look, you can see his tattoo; we did it yesterday."

Inside the ear was a serial number that identified the puppy and his lineage.

Roli kept complete records.

"Does he need shots?"

"No, he can wait until he is in America."

16.

"Have you ever sent a puppy to the United States?"

"No, the furthest distance so far is Greenland. But we now have a few inquiries from the States."

"Will he need to be quarantined?"

"I do not think so, but the U.S. embassy will be able to answer importation questions."

"Are they good family dogs?"

"Yes, they are wonderful with children and protective."

His love for the dogs was contagious. All of his information was helpful, but it did not give me a basis for deciding. The decision would come from my heart.

We spent an hour playing with the dogs and could have stayed the whole afternoon, but Roli had to leave to go to work.

"Would it be OK if we came back?"

"Come back anytime, and as often as you like."

"I like the one with the purple collar." All of the puppies in the litter had Swiss names beginning with the letter *B*, but since I could not pronounce most of the names, the collars became my means of identification.

"I'll save him for you."

I left with a warm, open feeling, and the urge to giggle at the pleasure of seeing such happy beings running about. The puppies' joy was contagious. Andrea and I felt like going to play on a hillside, to bask in the warm afternoon sunshine and chew on a shoelace. As I calmed down, I thought, "What am I getting into? Do I really want a dog?"

During the next few days, Bernese puppies tumbled through my mind. I thought another visit would help me to decide. When we arrived, Roli showed us to the puppies in the backyard and left to finish his chores about the house. It was difficult to be sure which ball of fur was which, as the collars were hidden under the hair; but one came over and began to pull on my shoe-strings. I picked him up, and sure enough it was Purple Collar. He was friendly, fearless, and so handsome.

We had been trying to think of a name for him, and now Andrea suggested Moritz. I thought she was thinking of San Moritz, but she was referring to the Max and Moritz in Wilhelm Busch's classic turn-of-the-century children's story, two mischievous characters.

Moritz . . . Moritz . . . yes.

Just like that, Moritz was named. However, name or no name, in the litter the purple collar was essential.

Pia arrived from her morning fitness run. She offered us some coffee and turned her attention to Deicha. She knelt down to talk with her, combed her, and gave her a treat. The puppies tumbled over one another to nuzzle Deicha for milk and Pia for affection. Patiently, she played with them; she talked to each puppy and hugged it against her chest.

"How do you decide if you will sell a puppy to someone?"

"I usually know if a person will be a good owner for one of our dogs. But if there is any doubt, I ask my children. You can't fool children; they see clearly."

"Will you sell me a dog?" After all, she didn't know me; she had no idea where Montana was; what my home was like; she had no opportunity to check my references.

Pia laughed.

"The children already approved you."

"Oh . . . thank you. Do you know which dog I should choose?"

"The minute someone comes to visit, I can see which dog would suit him."

She was not boasting; she simply trusted her intuition.

"Would you tell me which dog is best for me?"

"You should decide."

"I am considering Moritz, uh, the one with the purple collar."

After a bit of coaxing — perhaps begging would be more like it — Pia said she could tell me something about Moritz. "There is a Swiss saying: He has a ghost of a woman in him."

I don't know how, at such an early age, she knew, but this is Moritz. He has a feminine sweetness, a gentle softness and kindness. Pia knew his character when he was only a few weeks old.

As it was obvious that she cared deeply and poured herself into each puppy, I asked her:

"How can you let go of them?"

"Ah, it is difficult, but I realize that after I give each as much love as I can, in turn each puppy gives such love to a new family."

Talking with Pia helped me to understand what raising a dog would be like, and the tenderness of the relation-ship. Yet I was afraid to say yes and asked:

"Can I come back one more time?"

"Of course. Moritz will be waiting."

I was still unsure, but the next visit dispelled all hesitation. I knew I would soon have a puppy. Moritz had chased off the demons of doubt. At twelve weeks, he would be old enough to travel. On that day, Andrea and I picked him up and took him to her parents' home to play on the grass. Moritz ran about with enthusiasm, and when we sat down for dinner he lay under the table and went to sleep. He was so at ease and comfortable, he seemed to make all of us breathe more deeply and relax.

The next day Moritz and I flew to Montana.

Embarking

I live in western Montana, on a small Alpine lake in the beautiful Seeley-Swan range, an hour's drive from Missoula. In mid-April, we arrived home to find two feet of snow in the yard and Lake Inez beginning to thaw. Moritz explored the trees, the lake, the snow, and my shoes while I read two dog training books by the Monks of New Skete: *The Art of Raising a Puppy* and *How to Be Your Dog's Best Friend*. I felt like a novice parent reading Dr. Spock. We began our life together sleeping outside on the screened porch.

Moritz was a twenty-five-pound bundle of soft black fur with big white paws, and deep brown eyes separated by his white blaze. He was affectionate and cuddly, and he already knew his name.

In the mornings we walked along a forested trail to the end of the lake. Moritz would run down the trail with his ears flopping and his hips swinging from side to side. If one wanted to see joy, Moritz was it. In the afternoons he would nap. He was friendly, fearless, and so naturally curious that he learned quickly.

After a month we enrolled in an eight-week obedience class that met Tuesday evenings in Fort Missoula Park. Amidst the frenzy of ten other puppies, mostly Labs and golden retrievers, it became apparent that Moritz was unusually calm. Unpredictable and excited activity did not disturb him. He maintained his alert, gentle composure through it all.

Moritz attracted people of all ages wherever we went. Of course he was a cute puppy, but the more I watched his interactions, the more I felt that something remarkable would happen. People just opened up when they saw him; talking, petting, hugging, and playing with him. With Moritz, people lost their self-consciousness.

One day I drove my friend Jerry to the Missoula Airport to catch his flight to Denver. We parked at the curb and started unpacking the station wagon while Moritz sniffed under a nearby birch tree. I called him to jump into the car, but he ignored the call, wandering from the birch tree to sniff at an evergreen hedge. I called again. Moritz lay down in the shade.

Jerry called.

No response.

Jerry looked at me, as if I knew what to do. Just then a well-dressed woman rolling her suitcase along saw our predicament, stopped, and said:

"You guys don't get it."

She left her suitcase, pulled up her skirt, climbed into the back of my station wagon, and with great enthusiasm began to call Moritz. He trotted over, looked at this stranger sprawled on the floor behind the front seats who was calling him, and jumped in.

I was speechless. The woman got out of the car, dusted herself off, straightened her skirt, and went to retrieve her suitcase.

"Excuse me, thanks, is there anything I can do for you?"

"No, you just did" — and she disappeared into the airport.

Moritz and I traveled everywhere together. We hiked, we went to town, we ate lunch on café patios, we gardened (Moritz dug, Barry planted), we visited friends.

His happiness and friendliness encouraged me to be less shy. Moritz would go right up to people who were fishing, eating lunch, hiking, reading a book, having a conversation, to see what was happening. Fortunately, in Montana, people are used to dogs and most love them, so he was welcomed. He was so fearless, so friendly and naïve, that people would stop whatever they were doing to enjoy him. He seemed to lift people's spirits. Maybe he was just a cute puppy, but I sensed that his calm composure was an additional draw.

I wondered if his presence might help more people. I remembered hearing about a program that trained dogs to visit patients in hospitals. I imagined that Moritz might be a good candidate.

The next time I took him in for a checkup, I asked the vet if she knew of any such program in Missoula. She gave me the number of STAR Dogs, which was affiliated with the Delta Society's Pet Partners Program. However, dogs had to be one year old before they could be registered. I waited until Moritz's first birthday and then signed up for the next all-day Saturday workshop.

The workshop began with a video of a Delta Society award ceremony, an HBO presentation hosted by Mary Tyler Moore. Just seeing the generosity and enthusiasm of the volunteers and their animals was inspiring. One woman had been bringing her pet Vietnamese pig, Harley, to visit a young paraplegic patient for over a year. I thought if a pig could do it, so could Moritz.

We were given a big instruction book to read. It laid out the rules for bringing animals — not just dogs — into the hospital. Our instructor went through it with us, answering our questions, e.g., what to do if the patient required immediate medical attention; what types of leashes and collars were allowed; the grooming of both the dog and owner; etc. Afterwards, she told me to fill out the questionnaire inside the book, and mail it along with a photo of Moritz and me to the Delta Society.

In two weeks, I would bring Moritz to the second part of the registration, the thirty-minute team evaluation test. This is to determine if the dog is predictable, reliable, and safe, and to see how well the dog-and-owner team works together. We had to pass the written questionnaire, previously submitted, and the team evaluation test before the Delta Society would register us. Once registered, a Pet Partners volunteer is provided with liability insurance up to $1 million when visiting hospitals, nursing homes, or other care facilities. This eliminates some of the financial and legal obstacles to bringing therapy animals into the hospital.

On Saturday morning Moritz and I went through the team evaluation checklist without much difficulty. He remained composed when confronted with loud noises, strange equipment, people in wheelchairs, being touched by half a dozen people at once, and meeting another dog. We passed. As soon as the paperwork was completed the Delta Society would notify us when we could begin. We celebrated with a long walk along the Clark Fork River.

I naïvely thought we were ready to go. Community Medical Center had requested therapy dogs and I called to set up an appointment. However, they had their own set of requirements. These included watching three more hours of videos, reading up on hospital procedures, and taking a TB test. The entire approval process, from the initial call to STAR Dogs to the reading of my TB patch, took three months.

The final step was registering with the Delta Society. I called to see where we stood in the queue. I had thought, by now, we would have received our approval and had scheduled our first visit. The Delta rep was friendly and asked me to hold on while she checked. A few minutes later she returned and said, "Funny — yours was the next application in the stack." "If we pass," I said, "could you fax the approval to me? We've got an appointment scheduled for tomorrow."

A few hours later, the fax arrived with a note, "Good-looking dog."

Visit 1

The night before our first hospital visit, I bathe Moritz. He looks fluffy and even bigger than usual. I wonder how he and the patients will react to each other.

We leave early in the morning. Our getaway is chaotic, as I search for everything we need for a trip to Missoula. Moritz knows we are going outside and follows me all over the house with his tug-of-war towel. After forgetting Delta Society's fax, my car keys, sunglasses, and my hat, I decide that this offers a challenge to improve my concentration. I try to remember what to take and where to go, and to plan the most efficient errand route around town. Moritz gallops across the lawn, full of energy and wanting to play. After some coaxing and a biscuit bribe, he hops into the car and we are off. (Yes, I needed a bigger car to accommodate him.)

We leave at sunrise, watching shades of pink and yellow touch the mountain peaks. When we slow down to pass through small towns, I lower the back windows. Moritz sticks his head out the window, his ears blowing in the wind and his nose sniffing the morning air. He personifies adventure. We don't often go to town; he must sense something is up.

We arrive as Missoula is just awakening. Missoula is a city of 75,000, home of the University of Montana, and in many ways a friendly college town, community oriented. The meter maids carry dog treats, as do the drive-in bank tellers and the city parking lot attendants. In fact, it's surprising how many stores give out dog treats. People ask if they can give Moritz a treat, and when given permission, seem to become as happy as Moritz — a testament to the mutual benefits of generosity.

We stop at the French bakery for freshly baked pastry and tea. Moritz sits outside next to the park bench, waiting for me to come sit down and eat. Even at this early hour, a few people stop to talk to him. We walk a few blocks to hike on the trail along the Clark Fork River. Moritz sniffs among the willows along the river, runs across the football field, and stops at every lamppost, while I watch the changing colors of sunrise on the river and mountains. Invigorated, I prepare to tackle the to-do list.

About thirty minutes before our appointment, we drive to Community Medical Center. The hospital is a modern three-story building, part of a larger campus with office buildings and a surgery center adjacent to Fort Missoula Park. We leave the car in the hospital lot and walk across the street to the park. It is well-manicured with four or five playing fields, a path for walkers, horseshoe pits, picnic tables, basketball courts, tennis courts, and Fort Courage Child Care Center. The ground crew is busy mowing when Moritz arrives, racing past second base into the outfield, whizzing past the lawn mower tractor. I wonder when the driver will stop and start screaming, "Get that dog off the field!" It never happens. He just waves and smiles and goes about his business. As for Moritz's business, the park provides handy mutt mittens and plenty of trash cans. We leave in time for our eleven o'clock meeting at the Activities Office.

Our liaison, Jessi, introduces herself. She explains that she is a substitute for Katie and Brenda, the regular staff liaisons who will shepherd us on our visits. I swipe my hospital identification card through CMC's security time clock as Moritz sits patiently looking down the hallway. Jessi asks us to follow her, and we begin.

As we enter the rehab section, faces pop up from behind the computers and a buzz begins. Moritz troops along beside me, alert, curious, and calm. Our first visit begins with Cody. He is ten years old. He sits slumped in an armchair, eating M&M's. His mother sits next to him. He has a brutal looking scar on his shaven head, his left arm rests in a sling, his right hand looks delicate but useable, and his legs slight, with big sneakers on his feet. He sees Moritz and opens his eyes wide behind his thick, steel-rimmed glasses.

As Cody reaches to pet Moritz, he begins to talk. Moritz nudges his nose against Cody's chest. The boy pushes his glasses back on his nose and, ever so slowly, becomes more animated. He begins to talk about his uncle's chocolate Lab, and works hard to pronounce "Moritz." His mother, looking tired and concerned, straightens up in her chair. She does not ask or seem to care how this big dog has found his way to her son. Cody, too, begins to sit up straighter to reach for Moritz, who now lies down by his chair. As Cody reaches forward, his M&M's spill over his lap and onto the floor. Moritz stays relaxed and does not move. Now Cody becomes really engaged. Moritz's calm seems to give him confidence, and he struggles to stand up and pet him. He wobbles up, his mother holding him at her side. He turns to his Mom and says:

"I don't need you to hold me!"

"For now, you do."

"Mom, can I have a dog?"

"No," she gently replies.

Cody is disappointed, but he seems to understand.

Cody responds to Moritz like a healthy youngster ready to play with his dog. Although he has been through an ordeal, his recovery is well under way. I think his Mom is shocked to see him stand up. Our visit may have tired him, but as we leave, he calls out:

"Are you coming back again?"

"Yes, we'll see you next Tuesday."

☙

We stop to see a cheery elderly man, Bob, who is coming down the hall in his wheelchair. His therapist is at his side, encouraging him. Bob calls Moritz and pulls him to his lap. He explains with a smile that he misses his own dog, who is waiting for him at home.

☙

We walk a few rooms farther and I hear Jessi ask the patient if we can visit. The patient replies, "I don't like dogs much, but come in." We are introduced to an attractive, red-haired, middle-aged woman whose right arm is in a splint and taped to the arm of her wheelchair. As Moritz approaches her, she looks up; then she stares.

"Could you find my glasses and give them to me?"

I say, "You don't need them. You really do see a big black dog, and it is true."

She laughs. "He's so pretty, I want to see him."

She cleans her lenses before placing them on her nose. As Moritz comes into focus, her expression relaxes. She leans forward to look closer and sighs.

Her husband, a gentle-looking man who reminds me of an Italian barber, walks into the room and she points to Moritz.

"Isn't he beautiful?"

Her husband reaches for Moritz and says:

"He sure is."

"Where did you find him?"

"In Switzerland."

"How old was he when you brought him home?"

"Twelve weeks."

"How much does he weigh?"

"About 80 pounds. When he's full-grown he'll probably reach 115 pounds."

"Does he eat much?"

"No, only two cups, twice a day."

While her husband asks questions, she continues to concentrate on Moritz.

I show them the markings of a Bernese mountain dog, and the tattoo in Moritz's right ear.

"We live in Butte. He looks like a real winter dog."

"Yes, he is; he loves the snow and cold weather. Bernese are used for mountain rescue work."

"Is he always this calm and gentle?"

"Yes, ever since he was a puppy."

The conversation is so warm; I hope we will have another opportunity to talk. As we turn to leave, the woman looks at her husband.

"I didn't want another dog, but maybe it's time." Both thank us for coming to visit.

꙳

As we check out of the hospital, Jessi asks:

"When do you want to come back?"

"Tuesdays are a good day for us."

"I'll talk to my supervisor and let you know."

"Was Moritz appropriate for your program?"

She looks surprised and says, "Are you kidding?"

We leave. I hug Moritz and thank him and take him to the park for a walk. He seems to have taken the visit in stride, all in a day's work, and now runs through the park to check out a small herd of cows in a neighboring pasture, chase a crow, sniff around the soccer goal, and race over the newly raked horseshoe pits.

Not much to it, just a day full of new experiences.

But our visit has touched me. Moritz is open and friendly, and that is the way everyone we met welcomed us.

Visit 2

Tuesday arrives quickly. We leave early to run errands and have time for a walk before going to the hospital. It takes about an hour to reach Missoula, and Moritz sleeps in the back of the station wagon, but once in the city, he is up and active, ready to follow his nose.

We walk in the park, and at eleven o'clock we meet Brenda Kania, our staff liaison. She is only twenty-five, but it is soon apparent that she has a gift for caring. She has chosen many patients for Moritz to visit today.

We begin with Gertrude, a frail woman of ninety. She sits in a wheelchair with her head down, reading a magazine. Brenda asks, "Would you like to see a big, beautiful dog?"

Gertrude continues to read her magazine. She mutters, "I don't care much for dogs."

Brenda persists. "He comes from Switzerland."

Gertrude looks up. "OK, bring him in."

When Moritz enters Gertrude's room, he goes directly to her and puts his nose on her nose. She is surprised, drops her magazine, and tries to speak, but her words come out mumbled. She stops and points to her throat, indicating that she is having trouble speaking.

I assure her that this is no problem.

"I'll tell you about Moritz. He's a Bernese mountain dog. I brought him home from Switzerland when he was twelve weeks old. He weighs about 80 pounds, but he'll probably weigh 115 when he's grown up. Bernese are used as rescue dogs and to pull carts in the Alps. He's gentle. He's a good family dog."

Gertrude listens to me, looks at Moritz, and relaxes. After a few moments, her normal speech returns. She speaks slowly but clearly:

"He's so big. He's so calm. Was he always gentle?"

"Yes, Gertrude. He's been this way since he was a puppy."

Gertrude reaches over to pet him.

"He's so soft, and his colors are beautiful."

Suddenly Gertrude seems to shed her years and her worries. She laughs and tells us about a dog that she had when she was a child. After a few moments she says, "Thank you" and returns to her magazine.

Rambling down the hallway in his wheelchair comes Bob, the cheery man we met last week. Bob calls, "Moritz!" Tail wagging, Moritz goes directly to him. Bob grins. He tells us that he is leaving as soon as his son comes to pick him up. He is eager to go home and gives Moritz an affectionate one-armed hug.

"Is Cody still here?" I ask, since I know he would love to see Moritz again. Sure enough, he's next. When we walk into the room, Cody's eyes once again open wide. In a week, Cody has improved. He is alert, his voice and enunciation are back, his energy is higher, and, except for his legs, he has better control of his body.

He is excited and talks and talks.

"Mom, can I have a dog?"

Patiently she replies, "A dog like Moritz is too big for our apartment."

"He could sleep with me."

"If he gets in your bed," I say, "there'll be no room for you. He weighs nearly a hundred pounds. How much do you weigh?"

"Fifty-two pounds, but I'm gaining weight."

"So is Moritz."

"Oh."

Cody points to his forehead and asks, "Can you see where the bullet went between my eyes?"

"Bullet?"

Dizzy, I turn to his Mom. "Yes," she says, "a bullet went through his forehead and out the back of his skull, but it didn't do much damage."

"Not much damage?" I say to myself. Is it possible? Can this be?

I hesitate in disbelief, take a breath, and begin to make small talk. I am so overwhelmed that I feel faint. A bullet into the head of a child? For the first time, I wonder, "Can I continue? Am I able to witness such suffering?"

All my life I've tried to avoid pain. In the past, as soon as I entered a hospital the antiseptic smell would make me feel queasy and lightheaded and I would start to sweat. As a child, I once went to the hospital with my mother to visit a relative. I remember my mother looking at me and saying with concern, "You are ash white. Do you want to sit down?" Thereafter, all talk of my becoming a doctor ended.

I wonder, "Have I made a mistake? Maybe I'm not

strong enough to help." Cody continues describing how he accidentally shot himself, the path the bullet took out the back of his head, the details of the operation, and the trap door the doctors made in the back of his skull. I take a deep breath and another, telling myself, "Keep going, breathe, and pay attention." Moritz helps me to overcome my fear, serving as an alter ego, fearless, friendly, and — most important — calm.

"Can I take Moritz for a walk?" Cody asks. His question interrupts my mental tailspin.

"You bet, but let's wait until next week when you'll be stronger."

Cody excitedly agrees, ready for the next challenge and looking forward to having fun with Moritz.

As I leave Cody, I feel sad. I wonder how such an accident could have been prevented. Brenda asks, "Have you been upstairs to the pediatric section? We have a few requests to come visit."

The third floor houses the pediatric and postoperative patients. Here, the environment is far more intense. Lots of doctors, nurses, and critical-care patients create a highly charged atmosphere. Moritz walks off the elevator, senses the electricity in the air, and lies down.

There is a sudden pause in the activity. One nurse approaches Moritz, kneels down, and begins talking to him. Others join her. Soon everyone is talking about dogs, or Moritz, and the environment is transformed. The tension dissolves as if the recess bell had rung, and the class had raced from their desks to go out and play.

Someone calls, "Barry!" and I turn to see my friend Laura. Her daughter is in the next room, recovering from an emergency appendectomy. Laura looks relieved to see a friendly face and smiles when she sees Moritz.

He wags his tail and Laura laughs.

Down the hall, we are invited into a warm, dimly lit room. A five- or six-year-old boy slumps on his father's lap. His bare chest is patched with monitoring devices and an IV is taped to his arm. He is barely conscious. When Moritz approaches, the boy does not react. His father tells him briefly about Moritz and asks him to pet the dog. He takes the boy's curled hand and puts it on Moritz's head. No response. Moritz lies down and waits. The father completely embraces his son. Although he notices us, he is one hundred percent attentive to his son. He looks exhausted, but his focus and genuine care make me feel at ease. It is as if all pretense has been stripped away; only his affection and care for his son remain. We try again to have the boy "see" Moritz, but this is not the time. The father looks up at me from behind his son's head to say, "Thank you for coming."

I quietly reply, "Thank you." I am so moved that it's all I can say. Later, I wish that I could have shared with him my feelings about his courage and honesty.

⌒

We leave the hospital. Moritz is subdued, either from the heat or from the two-hour hospital experience. We walk to the park. As soon as I unsnap the leash from his collar, Moritz takes off. He darts toward a father and daughter who are having a picnic. There is a large McDonald's sack on their blanket. Full speed, he races toward them. The girl laughs at him, making no move to protect her French fries. Her father looks more apprehensive but allows the scene to play out. Moritz stops at the edge of the blanket and sits down, awaiting some morsel of food. When nothing is forthcoming, he runs full speed across the grass, free as a bird, with an elegant gait and the white tip of his tail in the air. I think he wiggles and dashes to welcome his freedom back.

Not so for me. I am numb. I cannot forget the scene of the father holding his son. I drive to the Good Food Store and buy a fruit shake to drink on the way home.

I don't feel like stopping anywhere — I just want a long drive home through the mountains to settle myself. I feel surprised by my own fear on this visit. For the first time, I noticed that I was holding my breath as I entered some of the rooms.

The patients' conditions vary widely, both physically and mentally. However, when Moritz walks into their room, he generally receives their full attention. His presence, his beauty, his nature and size, lure people to him. For a few moments the patient seems relieved from the burden of being ill. I cannot evaluate the meeting from the patient's perspective. From my side, I feel humble.

Visit 3

Today's visit has been changed to 2:30 in the afternoon. This disrupts our routine. Usually after the hour's drive from home, we take a long walk along the Clark Fork River for some morning exercise and fifteen minutes before entering the hospital we walk in the park. Today I am rushed and Moritz is stuck in the car, except for a brief run around the well-groomed lawns of Wal-Mart.

He is bursting with energy when we meet Katie MacMillen, our staff liaison. Katie alternates each week with Brenda to lead us on our rounds. She tells me that Gertrude has asked to see Moritz again, but she won't be available until the end of the hour. Katie has a wonderful sense of humor, and she knows dogs. She gently grasps Moritz's head and looks into his eyes. "So," she says, "you're ready to go, are you?"

We begin in the maternity ward, with a visit to a sixteen-year-old girl. A high-risk pregnancy will keep her on bed rest for four months, until her baby is due. Her love

for dogs nearly catapults her out of the bed when she
sees Moritz. Here is a big distraction from her boredom.
She talks and talks; Moritz lies down. The phone rings,
she talks; back to Moritz, she talks; the phone rings, and
she talks. Teenage energy confined to bed. I wonder if
Katie, seeing Moritz's energy, has deliberately matched
these two. We excuse ourselves as, once again, the
phone rings.

☞

We are waiting outside the elevator in the pediatric
section, about to go to the next floor, when a house-
keeper stops and kneels down in front of Moritz. He
sits looking directly into her eyes, and she hugs him
as if they were old friends.

"Shake hands."

Moritz's paws remain on the floor.

"I'll bet you don't do those stupid tricks, do you?"

Unperturbed, she reaches into the pocket of her smock
and pulls out some homemade dog biscuits. Moritz sits
up and she feeds him. On future visits, whenever we come
to the pediatric section, Moritz will look for her. If she's
not there, he'll wait to see if someone else will go to the
kitchenette for biscuits. Usually a doctor or nurse will
take the time to find the treats and give him a few.

We are invited into a room with a three-year-old boy, whose mother has just woken up in the chair next to him. The boy lies spread-eagled on his bed with a cobalt blue cast from his hips to his toes. He looks lost in his adult bed, his chest pasted with patches connected to monitors. An IV drips clear liquid into a vein on the back of his right hand. His nose is stuffed with oxygen pinchers; his blond hair is in a Mohawk with a white gauze bandana around his forehead. He looks scared. The scene is unforgettably surrealistic: the cobalt blue cast, the plastic IV tube and bags, the green zigzags on the monitors, and the boy's blond hair shooting straight up from his skull.

He cannot speak, and cries a little. He seems in pain; perhaps he is sedated. We go around his bed so he can touch Moritz with his free left hand. Moritz puts his nose against his hand, his chest, then goes nose to nose. The boy squirms and cries. Moritz, his tail wagging, calmly remains near his face. For a few seconds there is silence. Immobile, unable to pet the big dog or push him away, the little boy responds with sparkling eyes. Then, amid the hum of all the monitors, and short of breath, he laughs.

His mother sees the connection, sits up, and begins to ask questions:

"How come he's so gentle? He's so big, but so calm.

"What kind of dog is he?

"Where is he from?

"How old is he?

"How much does he weigh?"

And then, "Thank you."

After we leave the room, I ask Katie:

"What's wrong with him?"

"He may have been born with a dislocated hip. The surgery would be to repair it. Or he may have been injured."

Katie expresses surprise at Mortiz's gentleness and composure.

"Is he always like this?"

"Yes."

"Does Moritz respond differently to different patients?"

"Differently?"

"Does he pick up the energy level of the patient? Some dogs seem to sense what the patient needs. Some put their paw on the bed, or really try to get the patient to respond. Some of them want to get on the bed."

I think for a moment.

"No, I don't think so. He seems to be the same with everyone; he doesn't do anything special. In fact, it may be his equanimity that is unusual."

When we return to the nurses' station, the nurse behind the desk looks up from her paperwork. No doubt it has been a busy morning for her. She looks tense and tired, but she takes the time to say:

"Thanks. You know, our staff needs his visits as much as the patients do."

⌒

We get on the elevator to return to the rehab unit. Moritz is accustomed to the elevator. However, he is still a surprise to the people standing inside the elevator. Frequently, they exclaim,

"How did a dog get into the hospital?" or "Gee whiz, what a big dog!"

Katie, unflappable, smiles. "Moritz is a therapy dog. He makes weekly visits to patients."

Magically, Moritz has been transformed from a big black dog contaminating the hospital with dog hairs to a valued member of the therapy team. He is suddenly treated with such respect, you would think he was the chief of surgery.

☞

A nurse stops us, introducing herself to share her delight that she is about to get a Berner puppy herself. Seeing Moritz has convinced her that this is the dog she wants. I congratulate her on her choice. She beams and returns to her desk.

☞

As we walk down the hall of the rehab unit, around the corner swings an elderly woman in a wheelchair, accompanied by two physical therapists. Moritz and she see each other simultaneously. "Come!" she calls, and he approaches her wheelchair. She throws out her left arm and hugs him, pulling him closer. He lays his head against her chest and she runs her IV-bandaged arm up and down his back.

I kneel down to look into her face. "Lady," I say, "you're brave to grab such a big dog without the slightest hesitation."

She laughs. "I've had dogs all my life. I love them!" As we part company, I turn to Katie.

"That was some meeting."

"Did you hear what the therapist said?"

"No."

"The patient's stroke left her with left hemiplegia and left neglect. That means that she doesn't feel or know that she has the left side of her body. Her reaction, the spontaneous use of her arm, was completely unexpected."

We look into Gertrude's room, but she has gone to therapy. We will try again next week.

⁀

Cody is our final stop.

"Morning, Cody. You're looking better."

"I am. I'm going home Friday."

His speech is perfect.

"Is that so?"

"Yes! I'll tell my friends all about Moritz." Moritz, sitting by Cody's wheelchair, hears his name and looks at Cody. Cody reaches over to rub his nose.

Cody's hair has grown out and his energy is high. Still paralyzed on his left side, he will require more rehabilitation. But he has recovered his high-spirited, mischievous, ten-year-old self.

His mother shows us the hospital's half page advertisement in Sunday's *Missoulian*. It describes Cody's gun accident and her search for the best rehab center in the state. The ad includes a photo of Cody and his Mom in a therapy session.

"Can I take Moritz for a walk?"

He seems eager to try something new. We have already been in the hospital for over an hour, and this is the time when we ordinarily leave for the park. Moritz, no doubt, is ready to go.

"Sure, let's go out into the hall and you can take him for a walk."

As I give Cody the leash, Moritz barks — a deep, loud bark. Heads pop up from behind the nurses' stations and out of the hallway doors. I lunge to quiet him.

A concerned nurse, a bit ruffled, comes over to see if Moritz needs anything. Cody bursts out laughing and begins to wheel down the hall with Moritz at his side.

After five or ten yards, Cody stops and Moritz sits.

"Good boy!" he shouts, smiling from ear to ear, his glasses sliding down his nose.

"Can Moritz come to my window so I can say goodbye?"

"You mean, go outside on the grass and look into your room?"

"Yes."

We go outside, locate the window of his room, and tap on it. His mother opens the window and Moritz sticks his head in.

Cody laughs and laughs.

"Goodbye, Moritz."

Visit 4

It is gloomy and rainy as we arrive at the hospital. My friend Lesley is visiting from Berkeley, and I have invited her to join us. Les is warm-hearted and social and she loves people. She says she wants to see how Moritz interacts with the patients.

The mood in the hospital feels heavy, as if the weather has dampened everyone's spirits. Brenda arrives, distracted and late. Her perfunctory attitude sets the tone for our visit. Moritz is subdued.

We begin in the rehab section. Our first patient is an eighty-five-year-old man. He sits in a wheelchair, resting his left arm on a clear plastic lap tray, a larger version of a child's high chair tray. He is alert and friendly. His wife sits in a nearby chair.

Above her head hang paper plates colored with crayons and cut to look like daisies. These simple works of art are warm and cheerful. Along the windowsill are vases filled with gladioli, sunflowers, roses, zinnias, and lupine. The artwork and the flowers make the room cozy.

"The paper daisies are beautiful," I say.

Both of them light up.

"Oh yes, those are from our granddaughters. The oldest is eleven and the youngest is five."

"How about these flowers? Are they from your garden?"

"Some are from our garden. Some are from our friends and neighbors."

"They're really beautiful. Congratulations."

"I'm Archie. This is my wife, Phyll."

"This is Lesley, this is Moritz, and my name is Barry."

Archie looks us over carefully.

"Moritz, come here."

Moritz goes to Archie's paralyzed left side. Unfazed, Archie directs Moritz to his right side and then scratches him behind the ears. Moritz sniffs for any food that may have fallen into Archie's lap.

Archie seems content to have him close. In an easy manner, he begins:

"I've had a stroke. I need this plastic tray to rest my left arm on, so it won't fall and bang into the side of the wheelchair. I'm retired from the bank in Libby. I was with the bank for forty-three years." He goes on to tell us stories of his career and family.

He is a charming man with a gentlemanly quality about him. He must have been a terrific banker. Phyll has probably heard the stories a hundred times, but she listens attentively.

When we stand up to go, Archie asks, "Will you come again?"

"Well, Archie, Moritz and I will be back on Tuesday, but Lesley is going back to California."

Archie looks disappointed. I think he finds Les more interesting than Moritz or me.

☞

I look back on this day and think that it seemed slow. Moritz mostly greeted the patients and lay down. Lesley may have been a distraction for him. Perhaps she was such a hit with the families of those we visited — especially with Archie — that Moritz sensed that he wasn't needed.

I never asked Lesley what she experienced during the visits. But a few weeks later she called to say that she had decided to volunteer once a week to read to grade school children in Oakland.

Visit 5

During the warm August nights, Moritz and I return
to the sleeping porch, since the cool pine-scented air
induces a good night's sleep. Moritz wanders in and out
through the dog door leading to the woods. One night,
around 2:00 AM, I hear the flap of the door and Moritz's
footsteps approaching my bed. Sometimes he will put
his nose on my arm or face to ask for some affection
before he curls up on his pillow. This time he puts his
nose on mine. I reach out from my sleeping bag to pet
him. Then I spring up and sink my nose into his fur.
There is no mistaking that odor. He has been skunked!
I turn on the light. Moritz looks sheepish and bewildered. My first thought is "Yikes!" We are due at the
hospital at eleven o'clock. I envision leaving a trail of
upturned noses as we make our way down the corridors.
Perhaps we will be suspended or expelled. While I fret,
Moritz sleeps. Finally, I calm down and fall asleep too.

I wake up early and remember that tomato juice is supposed to neutralize skunk odor. But I'm not sure if I

would have the courage to cover him with tomato juice
— besides, I don't have any. Under the garden hose,
I apply dog shampoo and scrub. Moritz resists; he does
not like baths. When we finish, Moritz is shiny, fluffy,
and well groomed, but a faint smell of skunk still
lingers on his fur.

"Oh, well, let's give it a try," I think, and off we go.

☙

At 11:00 AM we meet Katie to begin our rounds. A few
minutes later Megan, Moritz's favorite sitter, arrives.
I have invited her to come and see Moritz in action.
Meg attends the University of Montana and is thinking
of becoming a vet. Neither Katie nor Megan mentions
the smell of skunk.

☙

Eighty-year-old Mary Jean lies flat on her back in bed,
recovering from a back operation. On the table next to
the bed stands a giant clamshell brace, looking as if it
had been fished from the sea.

Moritz greets her by laying his chin on Mary Jean's
hand. She is a friendly woman with gracious social
skills. Her windowsill is filled with get-well cards and
fresh flowers.

Moritz lies down by her bed.

"This back contraption really hurt last night," she tells Katie. "This morning we found they had put it on backwards. How do you tell the front from the back?"

Katie picks up the brace, inspects it, and shows her the difference.

"Gee, Mary Jean, that must have been uncomfortable."

Mary Jean laughs.

"Once is plenty. Could you have someone shampoo my hair? It's a mess."

"Of course."

She asks for a few toiletries, and Katie assures her that she will take care of everything.

"Thanks Katie, I appreciate it. I'll have to learn to be patient while I heal."

⌒

Next, Archie's room. He is asleep in his wheelchair, but he wakes up when we come in and smiles when he sees Moritz. The room is filled with more flowers, cards, letters, and artwork. Phyll is sitting in a chair. She smiles to see us. Judging from all the get-well gifts, I am sure that Arch was not only a terrific banker but also a valued friend.

Moritz goes to the wheelchair and lies on the floor. In a minute, he rolls over on his side, sound asleep.

Archie isn't offended. "That's fine with me. That's exactly how I feel."

"Who's taking care of your garden?"

Phyll says, "I went home one day this week to pick up all the mail. But I don't worry about the house or garden. Our neighbor looks after the place."

Archie explains:

"That would be Monte, short for Montana. She's ninety-four. In the winter, if our snow isn't shoveled by 10:00 AM she clears the walk herself. If we go away, we ask her to look after things. This time, when I asked her to water the fuchsias in the hanging baskets, Monte said not to worry; whenever she sees our car gone for a day or two, she waters everything. She even uproots our dandelions."

"Archie, you're a banker. Do you think your world is bigger than the houses on your block?"

"It doesn't need to be; it's such a nice block."

He studies me.

"What else do you do besides visiting the hospital?"

"I've been an investment advisor and now I'm writing a book about my hospital visits. You might be in it."

"Well, if I am, I won't buy the book." He laughs, reminding me of Groucho Marx's line, "I wouldn't join a club that would have me as a member."

"I'll be here for another week. Could you stop by again?"

"Sure, we'll be back. By the way, do you smell a skunk?"

Phyll smiles knowingly.

"I thought I smelled a skunk," she says. We laugh and Archie begins another story:

"That reminds me of a girl I once dated who wore a skunk jacket — until it rained."

☞

As we continue our rounds, we see a tall man coming down the hallway. He moves like a stick figure, all stiff joints. My first thought is "Here's another test for Moritz." During the team evaluation, he was tested to see how he would react to strange-looking people. But this man is not testing; he is returning to his room from a physical therapy session. He spots Moritz and stops to pet him. He bends straight over from his waist, arm extended, like a crane. It is a stiff physical gesture, but gentle. Moritz greets him, attentive throughout, as the man pats him awkwardly on the head. The man seems to gain confidence; he walks around Moritz to pet him some more. He seems relieved — whether to be able to move around, or perhaps to be accepted without judgment. I see him relax ever so slightly before continuing down the hall, as if this encounter had been an ordinary event, nothing special.

On our way out of the hospital, Katie remarks in an oh-by-the-way tone that the faint skunk smell was not too bad.

Visit 6

Today in the pediatric unit we meet Bryce. He looks like a ten-year-old Huck Finn with an overgrown crew cut, probably as a result of his hospital stay. His left leg is bandaged from hip to toe and his elbow is taped as well. He grabs Moritz behind the ears to pull him closer. Then he begins to tease him. Moritz escapes, checks out the food on Bryce's tray, and lies down. Bryce looks up from Moritz to me, and says:

"I was hit by a truck."

"You're kidding?"

"No, it's true. I was on my bike. I wasn't looking and cut out onto the street. Bam! My leg was broken in a few places. I've had three operations. The last was plastic surgery on my leg. Can you tell?"

"No, I can't tell. Your leg looks good. How is the poor truck driver?"

His head drops. "I told him again and again it wasn't his fault; it was mine."

Bryce's aunt, who is in the corner of the room repairing a model airplane, adds, "The man hasn't slept for two or three nights."

Bryce looks sad. "This accident has slowed me down," he says, "but I think it's even worse for the truck driver."

⁓

We walk down the hall to a room where a frail nine-year-old boy lies on the bed with an IV in the back of his left hand. His name is Daniel. His grandmother is lying on a bed next to him. He wears big steel-rimmed glasses, which slide down his nose when he looks down to see Moritz. His smile reveals a wide gap between his front teeth. As Moritz approaches the bed, he comes alive. Jennifer, his physical therapist, follows us into the room and asks Daniel if he would like to sit up. "Yes," he says. "I want to see the dog." She gently puts her hands under his back and lifts him into a sitting position on the edge of the bed with his feet dangling over the side. She sits next to him with her hand on his back and I sit on his other side. Daniel seems pleased to be sandwiched between us. He sits up straight, looking down at Moritz.

"Daniel, this is Moritz. He is a Bernese mountain dog from Switzerland."

"How old is Moritz?"

"Eighteen months."

After a moment of silence:

"How old is Moritz?"

"One year, six months."

"Oh. Moritz and I are almost the same age."

Hmmm, Daniel is a sharp young man.

"Daniel, you're right. You must be a good math student."
Daniel ignores the compliment and fires his next question:

"How old would I be now if I were a dog?"

"What do you think?"

"I do not know."

"You would be sixty-three. Because as you know, you multiply a dog's age by seven to find how old he is in human time. So your age, nine, you multiply by seven, and that equals sixty-three years old."

"Oh . . . How much does he weigh?"

"One hundred pounds."

"Oh my," Daniel whispers. "How much did he cost?"

"About a thousand dollars."

"Really!"

"Oh my . . . I would have to work a long time."

"Yes, indeed. Not only that, it costs ten dollars to pet him." Daniel laughs and laughs.

"I can do twenty dollars' worth."

⌒

I look at this sensitive, intelligent child. His knees are swollen and he quivers suddenly. This quivering is barely noticeable, but Jennifer asks:

"Are you OK?"

"Yes, but I hate that. It scares me," says Daniel softly.

There is pain and frustration in his voice, but he is so polite and soft-spoken that I can hardly detect his fear. He lies back in his bed, and Jennifer takes out a goniometer to measure the range of motion in Daniel's knee. As she measures, Daniel and I continue our conversation. He lives in Great Falls and will be going home soon.

I notice that, unlike most of the patients we visit, Daniel does not have the television on. He does have a large-screen Nintendo game, but it too is turned off. His grandmother says that the game is a big help; Daniel is so unusually curious and intelligent that he could easily be bored, and the Nintendo keeps his mind occupied. But what seems extraordinary to me is that with a body too fragile to walk, he remains keenly (to my mind, courageously) engaged with life.

As we leave, he and his grandmother thank us.

"I wish we had more time together," I say.

"I thought you were coming back to collect your money," Daniel shoots back.

"Don't worry, Daniel, I'll find you. Moritz will track you down!"

Outside his room, I stop and ask Brenda:

"What was the spasm? Why is he in the hospital?"

"His spine is weak, and sometimes the energy in his body creates spasms. Daniel has cerebral palsy."

Visit 7

All week I think about Daniel. I am saddened and bewildered as to why no cure has been found for this disease. I remember that the Shriners Hospitals for Children are dedicated to children stricken with cerebral palsy and other crippling diseases. Searching Shriners.com, I find their mission statement:

> Provide the highest care to children with neuro-musculoskeletal conditions, burn injuries and certain other special health care needs within a compassionate, family centered and collaborative care environment
>
> Provide for the education of physicians and other health care professionals
>
> Conduct research to discover new knowledge that improves the quality of care and quality of life of children and families

This mission is carried out without cost to the patient or family, and without regard to race, color, creed, sex or sect.

All I can think is "Thank you, Shriners. Thank you so much."

⌒

It is Katie's week to be our liaison. "Katie," I say, "have you met Daniel?"

"No, who is he?"

As I start to tell her about Daniel, Jennifer rounds the corner, and I break off to ask:

"Is Daniel still here?"

"No, he went home."

"We had such a tender meeting. I hoped to see him again. I wondered all week about cerebral palsy and Daniel's life."

"He definitely is unusual," says Jennifer. "He's so bright. His grandparents took over raising him when he was six years old, because his parents were abusive. One would never know, seeing Daniel's shining presence, that he had such a difficult life."

Such a short visit — ten minutes or so — and Daniel has made an indelible impression on me. I wish I could have done more to help him.

⌒

The rehabilitation gym is filled with all kinds of equipment to help patients to regain their physical skills. We pick our way among the stairs, handrails, and parallel bars toward a middle-aged woman who lies, eyes closed, on a tilted board. Her face is expressionless.

"Claire," says the physical therapist, "open your eyes for a beautiful surprise."

Slowly Claire opens her eyes. Seeing Moritz, she tries to sit up and touch him. Her arms are slight and her hands and fingers curled in, but when she feels Moritz's head and pets him behind the ears, she seems to wake up and reaches out to hold him. She places her hands around Moritz's head and he moves toward her. Encouraged, she bends forward to scratch his back. She has great difficulty moving, but it is apparent that Moritz has motivated her. After a few moments she grows tired and lies back, closing her eyes. Katie smiles as we continue to the next room. She tells me that this is the first time that Claire has said yes to her recovery process.

⌒

We enter a sunny, yellow room, to find a bright-eyed woman sitting in a wheelchair. She points to Moritz and proclaims, "That's why I'm in the hospital!"

She had tripped over her dog, and broken her right shoulder and arm. She seems to hold no grudge against dogs and calls Moritz, who trots over to be petted. She pets him with her left hand while she tells Katie about her newest diagnosis — a broken neck. She is waiting for her doctor to come and discuss neck surgery.

"I'm not having surgery. I'm ninety years old, and I have two or three years left. I'll be fine, even with a broken neck. Being in the hospital has made me sick, not well. I'll feel better at home." She is a high-spirited, self-reliant, clear-headed woman who knows what she wants, and probably does what she wants.

"Where do you live?" I ask.

"I live in Missoula, but I grew up on a farm." She looks at Katie and says, "I'm waiting for my son to bring me some well water. I'm about out. I don't want to drink the city water."

She gives Moritz a pat on his nose and sends us off.

⌒

Archie sits slumped in his wheelchair.

"Archie, you don't look well. Is there anything we can do?"

"Oh I'm all right. Last night I slipped and fell in the bathroom and broke my rib." He grimaces in pain and with his right hand touches his broken rib. His paralyzed left arm rests in his lap.

"It's the darndest thing. I broke a rib a few years ago when I slipped on a step and landed on a lawn chair. It dug right into my side. I really howled. It was the most painful injury I ever had. It took a long time to heal. The doctor showed me the X ray of my rib cage and you could clearly see the old injury. The new one isn't supposed to be as bad."

Once Archie begins his story, he seems to forget his discomfort. He weaves a compelling tale; he's a natural storyteller. He wears gray slacks with broad blue suspenders, a striped shirt, and white sneakers. Although his suspenders are loose, I snap one.

"Arch, you really look like a banker today."

He smiles.

"How about a loan?"

Immediately his right arm shoots straight down, his index finger pointing at Moritz.

"Collateral."

"Moritz, collateral? Arch, how could you!"

We laugh until he exclaims:

"Please don't make me laugh. It hurts too much."

Visit 8

Bernese mountain dogs are accustomed to Alpine temperatures — warm summer days and cool nights. They take to cold, love the snow, and are undaunted by steep, mountainous terrain. It's no wonder they have become winter rescue dogs.

Our home at Lake Inez is a good environment for Moritz. Summer temperatures are usually in the seventies, cooling to the forties at night. When Moritz is too warm, he wades into the lake — not to swim, but to snap his jaws in the water to drink and cool off. I always thought it was an odd method of drinking until I saw him in the winter, snapping at the snow to quench his thirst.

August temperatures in Missoula are ten degrees warmer than they are at the lake, rising to the nineties by midafternoon. On hot days, Moritz is uncomfortable and breathes heavily. To escape the heat, we schedule morning visits and return home after lunch. If it is too warm in a hospital room, he will lie by the door on the cool linoleum.

By now we are familiar with the hospital and most of the staff. On each visit, Moritz is welcomed as an old friend. Today an elderly woman standing by the nurses' station sees the nurses petting him. She looks twice and says, "Golly, what a beautiful dog." I can see her thinking, "Big dog, what's he doing here?" She pauses, unable to contain herself, and blurts, "What's he doing here?"

I reply, "Isn't it surprising how good looks can get you into most anywhere?"

⌒

A ten-year-old boy is lying in bed attached to an IV, surrounded by his grandparents and his mother. He seems alert, watching television. Moritz greets him with his nose on the boy's IV hand. The boy pulls back. Immediately, his grandmother starts talking about dogs, and continues talking for most of our visit. The boy returns to watching television; so much talking doesn't give him a chance to connect with Moritz. However, I feel heartened by the plaque on the Nintendo console hanging from the ceiling: "Donated by Best Buy." I wonder who at Best Buy initiated such a generous gift.

⌒

We return to the first-floor rehab section. We are on route to another of its pastel painted rooms, when a physical therapist approaches us. She asks if we will go to see John in room sixteen. She says that John saw Moritz in the hallway and remarked, "Now that's therapy! I'd like to meet him."

Room sixteen: John is lying in bed on his side, waiting for Moritz. Moritz places his head on John's shoulder. John touches Moritz tenderly and sighs.

"I bred golden retrievers for years. Wonderful dogs. I had a good time with them. I still miss my dogs."

"How come you stopped?"

John doesn't answer.

"We did it for a number of years," he says after a minute, "and now my daughter owns Labs and goldens. She's the family dog owner now. We have a cat."

He begins to talk about his cat, but his heart is not in it.

I interrupt. "It's OK" — he looks at me — "you prefer dogs."

He pauses. "Yes. I prefer dogs."

John is probably in his seventies. Lying there in his gray T-shirt, he looks like a well-trained athlete. He is articulate and alert. He appears to be a self-reliant man, an outdoor person with a powerful will. In the midst of our conversation he stops, and takes a deep breath.

"I never expected to be sick."

My impression is that he is strong enough to be asking the hard questions. What happened? How could my body fail me? What's next? How long will I live? To combat his fears, he considers his options. Yet I sense that there are still deeper questions that he wants answered.

Undoubtedly, John realizes that his recovery will take time, and he will not find it easy to be patient. Already he feels ready to go home.

"How often do you come to the hospital?"

"Every Tuesday."

"Unfortunately, I'll still be here next week. Would you please stop in again?"

⌒

We enter a dimly lit room, bare of flowers and cards. In the back of the room a middle-aged man lies staring at two triangle grips suspended from the ceiling. His breath is short and shallow.

"Good morning, Jim. Would you like to see a beautiful therapy dog? He's big enough to reach your bed," Katie calls.

He remains tense and motionless, barely turning his head to see who is talking to him. Moritz begins to walk to his side, but suddenly backs away and lies down on the floor. As he usually touches the patient's arm or hand, his reaction surprises us.

"Moritz," I say, "stand. Come on, Moritz, get up." He looks up but stays down.

Jim remains in his own world.

Katie leans over his bed and looks into his eyes. "I know you are in pain. I can see you are doing a good job managing it."

With this, Jim begins to talk. "The doctor told me my nerves are exposed, like an electrical cord with all the insulation stripped away. He says that in time I should heal. It's plenty scary in the meantime, though."

"I know a woman who had Guillain-Barré syndrome and has recovered. Would you like me to call her and ask her to come see you? I'm sure she'd be happy to talk with you," says Katie.

He lifts his head from the pillow. "Yes, I'd appreciate a

talk with someone who's gone through this. I have so many questions."

"I'll arrange a visit in the next few days."

After we leave the room, I ask Katie to tell me more about this syndrome.

"You can see how painful it is; just the slightest touch can be excruciating. There may be a few random symptoms, but in the beginning it's easy to overlook them. Then suddenly the body just stops working, and it's baffling because you have no idea why. Fortunately, most patients do make a full recovery. You can find out more from the Guillain-Barré Web site."

"Did you notice? Moritz never touched him."

⌒

Our final visit for today is with a fit, middle-aged man who sits on the edge of his bed to welcome Moritz. His room is filled with flowers, cards, balloons, and two toy industrial cranes.

Pointing to the Tonka-sized cranes, I say, "Looks like you have a few special gifts on the windowsill."

He smiles. "Oh, those. My pals at work sent them over for repair. I fix heavy machinery for the railroad."

This modest man would probably fix anything with a smile. Judging from all the gifts in the room, many people care about him and miss him.

In an easy manner, he begins his story:

"I was diagnosed with a brain tumor. At first, I just felt pain in my back and had trouble walking. After they did a lot of tests, they found the tumor. Now I'm getting radiation treatments and learning to walk again. I'm going to walk into Washington Football Stadium on September 15th for the opening game. I promised myself I would do it. I have six weeks to get ready."

He shows us his prize possessions: a University of Montana Grizzly jacket his son has sent him and a 2002 football yearbook autographed with a personal message from Coach Joe Glenn, given to him by a friend. I can see him dressed in his U of M apparel, among 16,000 people entering the stadium. Inconspicuous, another Griz fan, one of the boys celebrating the opening of the football season. In much the same way he makes machinery work, he will quietly fix himself, nothing special.

⌒

As we are about to leave the hospital, Moritz walks, unannounced, into a room. Usually Katie or Brenda goes before us and requests the patient's permission to visit. This time Moritz leads the way.

Sitting on the side of her bed, facing the doorway, a woman in a hospital gown is eating a sandwich. Moritz approaches and then sits at her feet. I quickly explain that he wanted to come in; perhaps he smelled the food. She laughs and tells us stories about her dog. She is so unassuming, talking and finishing her lunch, and Moritz is so relaxed, sitting at her feet, that one would think they were old friends. As we start to leave, she looks at Moritz and says:

"Thanks for stopping in."

Visit 9

The first days of fall bring cooler temperatures and a crisp morning air. The colder it gets, the more energetic Moritz becomes. He embraces the change of seasons.

Early in the morning on our way to Missoula, Moritz and I stop to walk at Big Larch Campground on Seeley Lake. The summer camping season is over; the campground is empty. It is a scenic hike, one that Moritz loves. He is fascinated by the wildlife. The shoreline is filled with reeds, long grass, and a beaver dam. Flocks of ducks feed just offshore, and often a blue heron or two is standing in the reeds. Moritz is not a retriever; instead, he just bounds along, stopping now and then to see what all his thumping will flush out of the grass. In the past, he has scared a deer, some quail, and, of course, waterfowl.

This morning, he forages around the shoreline, sniffs the mud, quickly drops his head under the water, and chomps. He emerges with a beaver in his jaws. The beaver is probably as surprised as I am. I have never seen Moritz hunt; he does not see well, and I don't think he has a great nose. Yet there he is with a flapping beaver in his mouth. I shout, "Let go!" He looks at me and I shout again. I am afraid that he will kill the beaver. He opens his jaws and drops the beaver back in the lake. The beaver, still in shock, slowly swims to deeper water. Moritz, filled with curiosity, wades out after it, and the beaver submerges. Moritz sniffs around and returns to the trail, looking as proud as someone who has just caught his first fish. I feel bewildered. There is enough killing of the beavers in these lakes; and yet Moritz is just following his instinct. As I sort out my feelings, I pick up our pace along the trail. In the end, I am pleased that Moritz obeyed — and I hope he didn't hurt the beaver.

It is a beautiful fall day. Katie greets Moritz warmly; they have become friends. We begin with the pediatric unit. We enter a dark room where a mother sits with a five-year-old child. The mother immediately remarks, "Oh, look, it's that lovely dog again." It takes me a few moments to remember them. They were in the hospital six or seven weeks ago. I can't recall the reason, but I remember thinking then that this mother was filled with an unshakable faith that her daughter would recover. The mother says now that her daughter has pneumonia but is feeling better. The child grins to show us the shiny new braces on her teeth while she sits on the floor to play with Moritz.

Next we visit Isaac and his mother. Isaac is nine or so with a mischievous look. The minute he sees Moritz, he is ready to play with him. He asks if Moritz can jump into bed with him, and I say, "No, better he doesn't learn that trick." So Isaac jumps to the floor and begins to tease Moritz. He grabs, pulls, pushes, and tries to trick him. Moritz endures the initial assault and calmly sits down. Isaac realizes that he has been outmaneuvered and looks closely at his opponent. His mother has carefully watched the interplay. She says:

"Isaac, he is bigger than you, but see how gentle he is? Look at his beautiful face. Look at him."

Isaac climbs back on the edge of his bed, looking down. You can see how much he likes roughhousing with Moritz. He seems so energetic and strong.

"He probably won't be in the hospital long," I comment to his Mom.

"We don't know what causes his seizures," she replies. She looks concerned. "We are waiting for the diagnosis. Thank you for bringing your dog."

Isaac adds, "Please come back again."

⁓

We return to the rehab unit. Here we meet Shelly, a
middle-aged woman with a patch over her right eye.
She slumps in her wheelchair. She calls Moritz to her,
but Moritz lies down by the door. She looks disappointed
but takes time to study him and concludes, "He's a cool
dog."

Her physical therapist asks Moritz to come closer. She
encourages Shelly to reach out and pet him. Shelly
touches his head and comes alive. She pets him and
whispers to him.

After we leave, I ask Katie:

"What's wrong with her? She seems to have some trouble with her coordination."

Katie says, "Someone shot her in the head."

Once again, the thought of a bullet in the head makes
me dizzy. But this time the feeling passes quickly.

⁓

We have been visiting the hospital for nearly three
months. Moritz knows the routine by now; but he seems
a bit bored. He often looks out the entrance doors at
the sunshine, and the children playing in the park.

Near the end of the hour, he is eager to go outside for a walk and so am I.

As soon as we leave the hospital I unleash him and he dashes to the park. He begins his park tour checking out the children at Fort Courage Child Care Center. The playground is filled with toddlers running about behind a chain-link fence. One child spots Moritz and shouts:

"Dog!"

Immediately, the children halt their games, jump from the swings, scamper out of the sandboxes, and run to the fence shouting, "Dog! Dog!"

A long line of children, fingers poking through the fence, call for Moritz. A teacher shouts, "Hands behind your back!" and like a row of falling dominoes, each child clasps his hands behind his back. As Moritz parades by, it looks like a troop of soldiers standing at ease under the review of a five-star general . . . except for the glee on the children's faces.

⌒

Every Tuesday for the past three months, Moritz and I have visited the hospital. From our first day we have been welcomed to the therapy team and made to feel part of the larger healing process. Everyone has welcomed

Moritz, on all the sections and floors, from the intensive care unit to pediatrics. Moritz walks down the hallway and wheelchairs stop; doctors with stethoscopes hanging from their necks bend down to pet or play with him; visitors ask us if we will stop in their relative's room; and cleaning staff park their carts to hug him. Warmth and caring seems to permeate this environment from top to bottom, and I think this helps patients to recover faster.

I wonder how all this was created. How were the Pet Partners programs introduced? How did these programs come to be such a wholesome influence within the hospital?

I call Jennifer Martin, the volunteer coordinator, a gracious, soft-spoken, young woman.

"Jennifer, could you tell me the history of the program?"

"The program began in 1997," she tells me. "In that year, the administration approved registered Pet Partners dogs. At that time, I was an activities specialist. Katie MacMillen and I began by taking the dogs (one cat for a short time) to the rehab unit. From there, we gradually began to take them throughout the hospital. There was some resistance in the intensive care unit. Even flowers aren't allowed in those rooms, so how could dogs be permitted? But as the therapists, nurses, and doctors learned more about the program and began to see the positive effect that it had on the patients — and on the staff, too — they came around.

"Now the program is well received. And it keeps growing. In fact, we have a therapy dog visit every day but Sunday."

"Do you have any scientific way to evaluate the program?"

"Yes and no. No, it's not scientific. Yes, we listen. I hear patients asking for more dog visits and I hear therapists report that the dogs make a positive difference in their patients. And the hospital administration really supports what we do."

⌒

Jennifer, Katie, and Brenda are modest about the success of the Pet Partners program. They are a capable professional team that has quietly succeeded in making therapy dogs an integral part of patient care at Community Medical Center. The benefits of this program extend beyond the patients to everyone at the hospital — and into the larger community as well.

From the volunteer's standpoint, the program runs so smoothly that after the initial testing and orientation, there is no paperwork, no bureaucratic red tape. It surprises me how much I enjoy these visits and how much I look forward to coming back each week.

I am not sure how Moritz feels. He is such a happy being wherever he goes. But I sense that he likes to work, he likes to meet people, and he thinks visiting the hospital is a big adventure.

Visit 10

Fall arrives with cool, crisp days and intermittent rain.
It's wonderful hiking weather. The summer tourists
have headed south and the aspen leaves and tamarack
needles are turning golden yellow. We hike to nearby
glacier lakes and up into the Bob Marshall Wilderness.
Moritz is a good hiking companion; he seldom wanders
far. He is protective, but so friendly that I don't worry
about our encounters with other hikers or their animals.
He weighs a hundred pounds, the largest therapy dog
at the hospital.

Today we begin in the pediatric ward. Off the elevator,
Moritz awaits his routine biscuit, and we begin. In the
first room, a young boy sits watching television. There
is an IV attached to the top of his head, and his arms
are in splints so he cannot scratch it loose. Moritz
approaches him quickly and puts his nose on the boy's
nose. For a long moment they remain frozen, eye-to-eye.
The boy appears unruffled. Moritz nudges him softly
with his nose and lies down. His mother wants to talk

and uses Moritz as an opener, telling us about their dog, and then expanding into her troubles with the boy's father. Her son tunes out and returns to watching television. We excuse ourselves and continue our rounds.

Back in rehab, we visit Luke, a big man sitting in a wheelchair with a ventilator at his side. A plastic pipe is attached to his throat, and the sound of his breathing reverberates throughout the room. At first, Moritz seems to frighten him. Moritz sniffs around the equipment and backs off a few feet. He sits and looks at Luke, who barely speaks, never taking his eyes off this big dog. He seems uncomfortable and depressed. It's easy to imagine that he's tired of struggling to breathe. The longer he looks at Moritz, the deeper he breathes. He begins to relax.

"Would you like to pet him?"

He nods yes.

Moritz moves closer. Luke waits patiently. Slowly, he extends his hand, allowing Moritz to come to him. He touches his ear with featherlike softness. Suddenly, I feel a lump in my throat. It is such a sensitive gesture that I nearly cry. Moritz responds, putting his head in Luke's lap.

Brenda and I watch them for a few minutes and I bend over to whisper in Luke's ear:

"Thank you for your kindness."

A few rooms down the hall, we stop in on Eric. He is twenty years old, a big, strong young man who hit a deer while he was riding his motorcycle. He is numb on his left side and slow to respond to us. He seems to have a brain injury. "I really like dogs," he exclaims, sitting up in his wheelchair and reaching for Moritz. He tells us all about his dogs.

I ask, "Were you wearing a helmet?"

"No, I never would."

"How come?"

"I don't believe in them."

"Even after your accident?"

"Nope. My cousin was killed on a motorcycle wearing a helmet, and I'm not about to use one."

He sounds defiant.

"I'll probably be on disability for the rest of my life. I have some brain damage that can't be fixed. I dream of getting back on my motorcycle and letting loose."

95.

"Are you sure you're really not willing to wear a helmet?"

"No helmet for me."

"Well, good luck. I wish you'd wear a helmet."

☙

As we wait in the hallway, some of the staff come up
to greet Moritz. When I ask if they have dogs, most
say they do. I'm surprised by how many of them have
St. Bernards, Great Pyrenees, and Newfoundlands.
Montanans must like big dogs.

☙

As we leave the hospital for our walk in the park, we run
into Archie and Phyll.

It's a pleasure to see them. Archie went home a few
weeks ago, and I have missed his stories. They seem
happy to see us, too. Archie is returning for a checkup.
I look to see if his suspenders are still on; he smiles.

"I can't do without them."

"You know, Archie, your room had more cards and gifts
in it than any other room we've visited."

Again he smiles.

"Did you drive all the way from Libby today?"

"No, we stayed overnight in Missoula for our appointment this morning. But let me tell you, the physical therapy in Libby is more strenuous than it is here."

I can see that his rehabilitation will take time, but he is patient.

Before leaving, he reminds me to stop by if I am ever in Libby.

Visit 11

In mid-November Moritz and I drive to Santa Fe to house-sit for a friend. After a month we return home. I've missed our Tuesday morning visits and I look forward to resuming our rounds.

Now that winter has arrived, the trips to Missoula are more adventurous. The morning temperature at 7:00 AM is often in the low teens. First we must get to the car. Because I have a steep driveway and a car with two-wheel drive, I have parked the car in a pullout on the highway. We must walk uphill in the darkness, through the snow and along the highway to the parking place.

Moritz leads the way up the driveway to the road, where he waits for me. I trail along carrying laundry, newspapers to recycle, a change of clothes, a capped cup of tea, his leash, and the car keys. The cold invigorates him, but causes me to contract. I wear boots, gloves, a hat, a scarf, a parka, and I stumble up the drive. He has his nose in the air, a bounce in his walk. Along the highway,

I call him to heel by my side; he doesn't. I keep a close eye on him. Fortunately, at this hour there is little traffic, so there is not much danger, just rising anxiety until we reach the pullout.

At the pullout, he lies down by the car as I fumble to find the keys. The car looks like a giant ice cube. The doors are frozen shut; to open the car takes a strong pull, accompanied by a guttural cry, HAH! My full attention is now on starting the car. I turn the key in the ignition, whispering, "Please start." As soon as it does start, I push all the defrosters and the car begins to warm up.

I scrape the snow and ice from the windows. Moritz lies down and watches me patiently, probably wondering what all the fuss is about. When the windows are clear, we jump in. Hoping that we are not stuck, I slowly accelerate onto the frozen highway. By now, perversely, I have begun to appreciate this little ritual; it is always a challenge, and calls for a flexible mind and body. Also, it helps to have a strong back for shoveling snow.

⌒

Today, we begin with a visit to Hank, a friend who had a hip replacement yesterday. As we enter his room, he is about to try to walk. He is standing, pushing up on the walker and taking small steps. Carol, his wife, follows behind him with a wheelchair. Hank is cheerful and determined, but looks pale. Carol keeps her eyes on Hank. Then she suddenly sees Moritz. She is surprised and declares:

"He's too big to be in a hospital room."

By chance, another friend's mother is down the hall recovering from a knee replacement, so we stop by to visit with her. She seems in good spirits, ready to go home tomorrow, and immediately calls Moritz. When he goes to her she hugs him and begins to talk about her German shepherd. The room is too warm and Moritz heads for the doorway. She tells him:

"I'm happy you stopped in."

After lunch, Moritz and I take a walk downtown. I am looking in a store window while Moritz is looking down the street at another dog. Two men who appear to be homeless approach us, and one asks:

"Can I pet him?"

He is a strikingly handsome man, bundled in a parka. His dark-brown eyes are riveted on Moritz.

"Of course; go ahead."

He kneels down and calls Moritz. He reaches to pet him, but Moritz suddenly stops and suspiciously backs away.

Surprised, I say, "He's friendly; try again."

As he reaches out, Moritz barks. He seldom barks. The man guesses, "It's probably the alcohol. He smells the alcohol on my breath and doesn't like it."

"You're right. If there were no alcohol he'd be in your lap, since you show so much affection for him." He looks up and our eyes meet. I say:

"I appreciate your honesty about why he hesitated. It wasn't you, it was the alcohol."

He looks closely at me.

"Can I hug you?"

We warmly embrace and he says:

"I love you," and leaves.

Visit 12

Digging out of the snow, I leave at 6:00 AM to run a long list of errands in Missoula before we go to the hospital. We take a quick walk in the park. Moritz heads across the snow-covered soccer field to a favorite spot, a clump of white birches. This short run seems to energize him, and he enters the hospital with a sprightly gait.

Brenda greets us and we begin in the pediatric ward. Moritz knows that this is the floor for homemade dog biscuits, so he goes directly to the reception desk and sits waiting for a snack. If, by chance, nobody gives him one, he will move to the kitchen doorway.

Today he receives a biscuit, but all the children are asleep so we head down to the rehab unit. Here we meet Chris, a twelve-year-old boy with a long scar across his forehead. He sits slumped in a wheelchair. His speech is slurred and his entire left side is paralyzed. He seems depressed, but seeing Moritz, he cheers up. He calls me Raspberry and laughs. His father arrives, a strong looking man who jokes with Chris but appears heartbroken and frightened. Moritz lies down as the therapist enters the room to take Chris to work out in the swimming pool.

I ask the nurse at the station what happened to Chris. She says:

"The first day of hunting season he picked up a gun, probably a .44 magnum. It was loaded, and he accidentally shot himself in the head. He's a youngster whose whole life has suddenly changed, and he's confused and depressed."

⌒

We head into the rehab gym, where a patient lies supported in a sling raised above the mat by a small crane. This allows the therapists to work on her without having to lift her body. From a distance, she looks like a two-hundred-pound baby swaying in a Snugli.

The patient's name is Anne. She is barely coherent. When she agrees to a visit with Moritz, she is lowered to the mat. She needs help to turn from her back to her stomach so she can touch him. She has little use of her hands and arms, and it's a tremendous effort for her to find a comfortable position lying on her stomach. She looks trapped in a body that no longer functions. I recall reading a book by the French writer

Jean-Dominique Bauby, *The Diving Bell and the Butterfly*.
Bauby suffered such a severe stroke that he could only
blink one eye to communicate. He wrote a beautiful
book in this manner.

In his earlier visits today, Moritz gave each patient a
quick greeting and then lay down. But with Anne, he
approaches her, puts his nose up against her nose, and
does not move. Anne grunts and says, "He smells like a
dog." Moritz backs away. The therapists help her to move
her left arm out from under her body to give her more
freedom. She makes a few attempts to pet him. The therapists see that she is tired and thank us for our visit.

When we leave, I ask Brenda, "What's wrong with her?"

"Anne is a cervical quadriplegic. The spinal cord in her
neck has been sheared or pinched. It's a very serious
injury."

Our final visit is with Rolf, an intelligent looking man
in his seventies. He has suffered a stroke but sits upright
in his wheelchair. Immediately he calls Moritz. As he
plays with him, I can see that he really likes dogs.

"Rolf, it would be good for you to have a dog."

"Do you think so?"

"Sure. It will keep your heart open. How come you don't have one now?"

"I live in a mobile home park. That's no place for a dog. My wife would love a dog."

He pauses and I can almost hear his mind clicking away.

"Our lives will change after my stroke. We have to move to where it's wheelchair accessible. No landlord wants a dog."

"Rolf, there are always reasons, or excuses. I see you with Moritz and I guarantee, a dog will not be a problem. He'll help."

He pauses. He seems to be struggling to hold back his emotions. Then he says:

"My wife will bless you for saying this. She's wanted one."

"So will you. Go ahead and get one and everything will be fine. I'll see you next Tuesday. You'll still be here?"

"Yes, I'll be leaving a few days before Christmas."

"Good. Get a puppy for Christmas."

"Goodbye Moritz, see you next week. Oh, yes, what's your name?"

Epilogue

Moritz and I have been visiting Community Medical Center for six months now, with a one-month break. I never imagined (1) that I would have a dog, or (2) that I would be taking a dog to visit hospital patients. Hospitals have always made me nervous. They were a piece of life that I avoided.

Moritz seems to have grasped the idea of hospital visits.

In July, we visit my friend Lyle Poncher and his family at Potosi Hot Springs Resort, in the scenic Tobacco Mountain range. Lyle and his kids, Amy and Zachery, have come here after five days of serious trout fishing. Kathy, Lyle's sister, and Diane, his mother, have joined them for a vacation. Lyle and I have been friends since college and by now I feel a part of his family. This is our time of year to be together.

Moritz and I arrive at noon to find everyone sitting by a hot spring pool, eating box lunches. The kids are shocked to see how much Moritz has grown in a year and are deterred from playing with him for about one minute. Then off they go, trying to get Moritz into the pool. After a while they begin playing with him more gently, and by evening they seem protective of him.

We sleep in two cabins, one for the men, and one for the women. Before bedtime, Kathy and Amy decide to sleep in a teepee, leaving Diane alone in her cabin. When Amy asks Lyle's permission to spend the night outside, he hesitates, not wanting his mother to be alone. But Kathy assures him that their mother will be just fine and Lyle reluctantly agrees.

Moritz is to sleep outside on our porch. I sit with him for a few minutes before I go to bed, looking at the star-filled sky.

Around 6:30 AM I wake up and go outside to check on Moritz. He is gone. I'm alarmed; Moritz always stays close. I call him. Silence. Can he be chasing a moose? More likely he went to the lodge to play with the other dogs. On my way to the lodge, I hear Diane's cabin door open, and Moritz bounds out to greet me. Diane, standing on the porch in her nightgown, explains that just before midnight she heard a low growl; then she heard Moritz scratching on the door, asking to come in. Once inside, he lay down on the floor beside her bed and went to sleep. Diane says that she felt he had come to look after her. She says she slept better that night than she has in a long time. Amy and Zach ask how he knew to go to her. Lyle shrugs. We look at Moritz, but he doesn't say.

⌒

Moritz's happiness seems like a contagious anti-disease. People are attracted to him immediately. They reach out to touch him, to give him affection, and to play. Initially, it may be his beauty they are drawn to, but later, they seem to appreciate his calmness.

He does not "do" anything special; no tricks; he doesn't even shake hands. Often he will just gracefully lie down. He is fearless and looks directly at you. He is equal to everyone. I have come to appreciate his patience, equanimity, tolerance, playfulness, kindness, and courage. In small ways, little by little, these qualities have rubbed off on me. One never knows where one will learn valuable lessons. In my life, a puppy from a village in Switzerland dropped in to share his goodness.

It's hard to measure the impact of our visits. It's certainly not just the patients who are happy to see him. Over the months, the hospital staff — doctors, nurses, therapists, volunteers, receptionists, and cleaning staff — have all welcomed him. A few reward him with biscuits; others pause in their work to greet him, hug him, or acknowledge his presence.

Patients smile, laugh, and confide in this unlikely bedside visitor. We treat each visit as a new beginning. Each doorway, each curtain we enter is fresh; we just go in and see what happens. I don't know how the patients feel after we leave. I do know that the visits touch me, either immediately or over time.

Tuesdays have become the high point of my week. Although I thought I was just the hand at the other end of the leash, the visits have affected me, bringing me face-to-face with illness, disappointment, sadness, and humility. They have removed some fear of the unknown and some of the ordinary filters between life and death. They have made me feel more connected to humanity.

Whoever created a park next to the hospital had a visionary idea. A walk in the park before, and always after, our visits allows us to return gently to the present. A falling leaf, the sound of the lawn mower cutting the playing field grass, the warmth of the sun, the smell of the morning air awaken my senses and I feel suddenly alive. On occasion, life, with all its contrasts and imper-manence, awakens in me a larger perspective, full of appreciation and gratitude. And wonder at the grandeur of it all.

Endnote

Oblivious to the obvious, I never realized until writing this book how much Moritz changed my life. His happiness is contagious, and is an anti-disease that helped me to heal. Perhaps, I did not realize his effect on me, as others may not as well; he does not really "do" anything.

He is calm, joyful, patient, open to life.

In the morning, I wake up and greet him, "Hello, Moritz," and his tail beats the carpet — seems like nothing much. Strangers stop to talk to him and we have a chance to talk, nothing much. Children run to pet him, nothing much. Patients ask to see him again . . . and so it goes.

Before long, I am overwhelmed with gratitude to be once again reunited so intimately with life.

Thank you, Moritz.

Nose to Nose was designed for Silent Moon Books by Eleanor Caponigro and set in the digital version of Linotype Didot.

It was printed and bound in Canada by Transcontinental Printing and Graphics, Inc., on recycled paper that meets library standards in paper permanence.

The drawing on the title page was made by Sally Sanders-Garrett.